BACKYARD BIRDS

Robins

by Elizabeth Neuenfeldt

BLASTOFF! READERS

BELLWETHER MEDIA • MINNEAPOLIS, MN

Blastoff! Readers are carefully developed by literacy experts to build reading stamina and move students toward fluency by combining standards-based content with developmentally appropriate text.

Level 1 provides the most support through repetition of high-frequency words, light text, predictable sentence patterns, and strong visual support.

Level 2 offers early readers a bit more challenge through varied sentences, increased text load, and text-supportive special features.

Level 3 advances early-fluent readers toward fluency through increased text load, less reliance on photos, advancing concepts, longer sentences, and more complex special features.

★ **Blastoff! Universe**

Reading Level

Beginners
Grade
K

READERS
Grades
1–3

Blastoff! DISCOVERY
Grade
4

This edition first published in 2022 by Bellwether Media, Inc.

No part of this publication may be reproduced in whole or in part without written permission of the publisher. For information regarding permission, write to Bellwether Media, Inc., Attention: Permissions Department, 6012 Blue Circle Drive, Minnetonka, MN 55343.

Library of Congress Cataloging-in-Publication Data

Names: Neuenfeldt, Elizabeth, author.
Title: Robins / by Elizabeth Neuenfeldt.
Description: Minneapolis, MN : Bellwether Media, 2022. | Series: Blastoff! readers. Backyard birds | Includes bibliographical references and index. | Audience: Ages 5-8 | Audience: Grades K-1 | Summary: "Developed by literacy experts for students in kindergarten through grade three, this book introduces robins to young readers through leveled text and related photos"–Provided by publisher.
Identifiers: LCCN 2021000682 (print) | LCCN 2021000683 (ebook) | ISBN 9781644874950 (library binding) | ISBN 9781648344039 (ebook)
Subjects: LCSH: Robins–Juvenile literature.
Classification: LCC QL696.P288 N48 2022 (print) | LCC QL696.P288 (ebook) | DDC 598.8/42–dc23
LC record available at https://lccn.loc.gov/2021000682
LC ebook record available at https://lccn.loc.gov/2021000683

Editor: Betsy Rathburn   Designer: Andrea Schneider

Printed in the United States of America, North Mankato, MN.

Table of Contents

What Are Robins?

Robins are a common sign of spring! These big **songbirds** are in the thrush family.

All in the Family

wood thrush

eastern bluebird

varied thrush

Robins have mostly brown and white feathers. They have orange chests.

Forest Life

Robins live in forests and fields. They live on mountains, too!

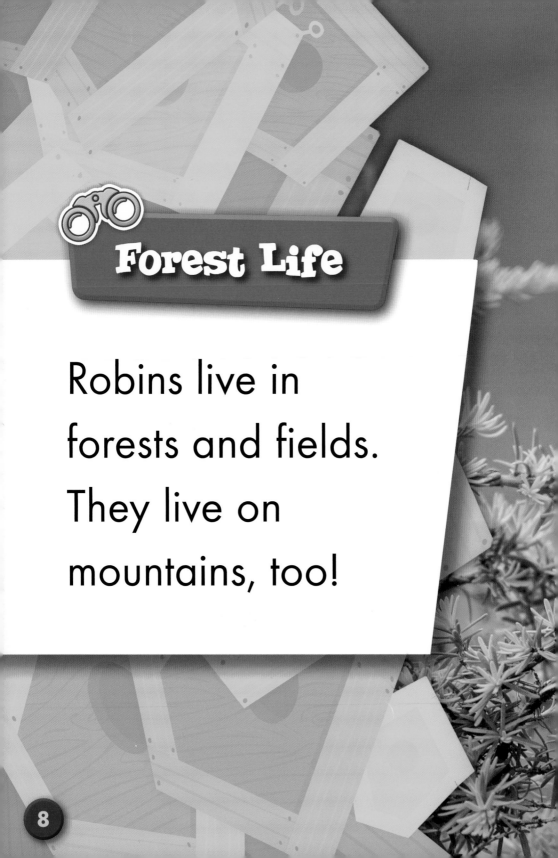

Robins build nests
in trees. Females lay
bright blue eggs.

eggs

nest

Robins find food on the ground. They eat worms, **insects**, and fruit.

Robin Food

worms   insects   fruit

13

Early Birds

Robins sing all day.
They start to sing
before the sun rises.
Wake up!

Robins are fast birds. They are strong fliers, too.

Most robins **migrate** in winter. They fly south in big **flocks** to find food.

flock

When it is warm,
robins fly north again.
Welcome, spring!

Glossary

flocks

groups of birds

songbirds

birds that make musical sounds

insects

small animals with six legs and hard outer bodies

migrate

to travel with the seasons

To Learn More

AT THE LIBRARY

Christelow, Eileen. *Robins!: How They Grow Up*. Boston, Mass.: Clarion Books, 2017.

Gray, Susan H. *Robin*. Ann Arbor, Mich.: Cherry Lake Publishing, 2021.

Murray, Julie. *American Robins*. Minneapolis, Minn.: ABDO Kids, 2021.

ON THE WEB

FACTSURFER

Factsurfer.com gives you a safe, fun way to find more information.

1. Go to www.factsurfer.com.

2. Enter "robins" into the search box and click Q.

3. Select your book cover to see a list of related content.

Index

The images in this book are reproduced through the courtesy of: PBallay, front cover (robin); IrinaKorsakova, front cover (background); FotoRequest, p. 3; cpaulfell, pp. 4-5; Johann Schumacher/ Alamy, pp. 5 (wood thrush), 16-17; Danita Delimont, pp. 5 (eastern bluebird), 12-13; Janet Horton/ Alamy, p. 5 (varied thrush); Willowpix, pp. 6-7; Top-Pics TBK/ Alamy, pp. 8-9; Chiyacat, pp. 10-11; Lost Mountain Studio, p. 11 (eggs); Andrei Metelev, p. 13 (worms); davemhuntphotography, p. 13 (insects); 84559255, p. 13 (fruit); William Leaman/ Alamy, pp. 14-15, 20-21, 22 (flocks); Animals Animals/ Animals Animals, pp. 18-19; BEJITA, p. 22 (insects); Tom Franks, p. 22 (migrate); Mucky38, p. 22 (songbirds); Mike Truchon, p. 23.